The House with Only an Attic and a Basement

ABOUT THE AUTHOR

Kathryn Maris is originally from New York and has lived in London since 1999. Her previous collections are *The Book of Jobs* (Four Way Books, 2006) and *God Loves You* (Seren, 2013), and a selection of her poetry appeared alongside the work of Frederick Seidel and Sam Riviere in *Penguin Modern Poets 5: Occasional Wild Parties* (2017). Her poetry has been published widely, including in *Granta*, *The Nation*, *The New Statesman*, *Poetry*, *The Best British Poetry 2015* (Salt) and *The Forward Book of Poetry 2017* (Faber & Faber).

KATHRYN MARIS

The House with Only an Attic and a Basement

PENGUIN BOOKS

PENGUIN BOOKS

UK | USA | Canada | Ireland | Australia
India | New Zealand | South Africa

Penguin Books is part of the Penguin Random House group of companies
whose addresses can be found at global.penguinrandomhouse.com

First published 2018
001

Set in 9.75/13.5 pt Warnock Pro
Typeset by Jouve (UK), Milton Keynes
Printed in Great Britain by Clays Ltd, St Ives plc

A CIP catalogue record for this book is available from the British Library

ISBN: 978–0–141–98657–9

www.greenpenguin.co.uk

MIX
Paper from
responsible sources
FSC® C018179

Penguin Random House is committed to a
sustainable future for our business, our readers
and our planet. This book is made from Forest
Stewardship Council® certified paper.

CONTENTS

'Identification is a highly important factor in the mechanism of hysterical symptoms; by this means patients are enabled in their symptoms to represent not merely their own experiences, but the experiences of a great number of other persons, and can suffer, as it were, for a whole mass of people, and fill all the parts of a drama by means of their own personalities alone.'

– Sigmund Freud

The Summer Day the Spike Went into My

The summer day the spike went into my
brother's head, as such things happened
in the twentieth century when the Freudian
death drive was often accessed out of
boredom, I learned from my doctor parents
that scalps bleed profusely. Twenty years later,
when Theodore and Cosima jumped on little
Robert's bed and Theodore fell off and his
white-blond head turned red, I said, 'Scalps bleed
profusely' and Rachel, his mum, thanked me
for my composure. Robert's mum, Emily,
who had wanted to be a jazz singer or actress
and who always introduced me as a poetess,
said she knew a couple who had a second child
because their friends' child died in a freak accident.
But back to the summer day the spike
grazed my brother's scalp: I slept beside him
in his racing car bed and my father woke me
and slapped my face, thinking, I assume, of sex,
whereas I was already thinking about death.

School Run

I board the same bus I boarded this morning
and see the same driver from the earlier journey.
Our eyes meet; he remembers me too.
When I exit, I feel abandoned by the driver

I know from many early-morning journeys
to my daughter's school in northwest London.
Why do I feel the driver has abandoned me?
Has an imagined intimacy developed?

At my daughter's school in northwest London
were the usual mums and dads I greet
with an imagined sense of intimacy
that has nothing to do with friendship.

Among the many mums and dads I greeted
with politeness, or something like fondness
having nothing at all to do with friendship,
were business people and psychoanalysts.

Out of politeness or something like fondness,
I do not ask the driver why he left me.
He's not in the business of psychoanalysis;
it's not his job to say I miss my *daughter*,

that it was a loss when my daughter left
my body, when I met her eyes after the birth.
It's not his place to say I'm losing my daughter.
I exit the same bus I boarded this morning.

The X Man

His superpower was that his testicles manufactured sperm
with exclusively X chromosomes & that was ironic because
not only was he a beast to women but his 40 baby girls grew
up seeking men like the father they barely saw unless they went
to his studio to be painted which wasn't OK with their mothers
who were not only jealous but guilty of giving birth to girls
who were products of an X chromosome-making monster
& would soon suffer at the hands of other monsters with X-
type sperm thereby assuring the continuation of suffering
& meanwhile all the girls became writers who slouched
from sitting at desks & being daughters & lovers of beasts.

ABC

Anne identified with Cate until it became a bona fide
illness, for Boris had left Cate, resulting not only
in psychic estrangement but an unconscious stream

of hostility directed not at Boris, but at his new woman,
Anne, whom Cate viewed as her rival. Cate remained
excessively tender with Boris, though Cate, for him,

had been a 'totem animal' from which he gained power
by 'eating'. Whereas Boris was the patriarch,
Anne was the ego alien; and whereas Cate was Anne's

fixation, Anne was no one's obsession, so she was
admitted to a psychiatric ward with the unbidden
associations she could not be induced to abandon.

On the rare occasions she slept, the manifest and latent
content of her dreams was the dance of abandonment
between Boris and Cate, which Anne, in her waking hours,

projected onto the walls, as though screening a silent film.
She could not be induced to abandon this footage;
she could not be induced to abandon her object love

of Boris (whose own object choice was his
ego-libido); or her identification with Cate, who felt
no friendship towards Anne. Soon Anne drew a mental

triangle on every surface she saw, be it phallic or
concave, and sometimes this triangle was isosceles,
sometimes it was equilateral, and often it was right.

Good Day

Do not be surprised
Reading my letter does not take much of your time
I understand you correctly
Looking for a girl you would like on the Internet
Looking for a woman for serious relationship
My opinion is the same as yours
I want to find a man perhaps even for marriage
If you want to play with me and my feelings
better not to respond to my letter
I'd like to find a sincere and loving man
I'm looking for a real man
I say this now so that later it was easier to communicate
A bit about me . . .
Irina my name . . .
I live in Russia . . .
I have permanent job and permanent salary
All is well in my life, with friends and parents
but there is no man who would love me
and it is hard for me to solitude
A lot of information is not currently the best option
I await your response and I'll tell you more
You can ask me any question
And now I have to go
Your letter and a story about yourself will please me if
you are looking for a Woman for marriage and serious
relationships
Postscript: I will answer some of your questions
I'm not looking for money or a sponsor for my life
I do not need your money, I have my own money
and even some savings
I hope I can find a single man who will never let me not hurt
Waiting for an answer
Your Irina

Case Study: Ms C

Ms C, 32, attended counselling with her father after discovering he was romantically involved with a woman her own age who bore uncanny similarities to Ms C in that they shared a birthday (a fact that seemed of significance to the patient), they had both attended Wharton, and both had worked for Ms C's father, a figure of international prominence in the hotel industry. Ms C described her reaction as 'devastated' when her father announced his intention to leave her mother, whom the patient described as 'a devoted wife for over 35 years'.

Ms C had no history of depression, and did not present with depressive symptoms. When asked if she believed herself to be depressed, she said she did not but that she believed that she had been 'replaced by an immigrant who had all of her attributes' and who would 'inherit all the money'.

Ms C was given further tests to rule out Capgras Syndrome and was advised to seek one-on-one therapy for future monitoring of her moods and delusions.

The House with Only an Attic and a Basement

'When two sane persons are together one expects that A will recognize
B to be more or less the person B takes himself to be, and vice versa.'
                    – RD Laing, *The Divided Self*

The woman in the attic did not have visitors.

The man in the basement gave parties that were popular.

The woman in the attic had mononucleosis.

The man in the basement had type 1 diabetes.

The woman in the attic listened to audiobooks which the man in
    the basement held in disdain.

The door to the attic swelled in some weathers; in order to shut, it
    had to be slammed.

'There is a way in which' was a way in which the man opened
    sentences,

as in 'There is a way in which to close a door so it doesn't slam.'

The woman in the attic took cautious walks to build her strength.

The man in the basement pointedly said, 'Some of us have ailments
    which are not manufactured.'

The man in the basement wrote stories about heroin.

The woman in the attic read stories with heroines.

The woman in the attic noticed a bruise that ran from the top to
    the base of her thigh.

The bruise looked like Europe.

The man in the basement was in love with the sister of the secretive
    man who loved him more.

He whooped at the woman, 'You killed your student?'

To himself he wept, 'I killed my father.'

The man in the basement, recently divorced, was left with literally
    two possessions.

The woman in the attic purchased books on psychopathology.

The man in the basement produced faecal matter

that blocked the pipes in both attic and basement.

The woman in the attic produced nothing at all.
The woman in the attic was a waste of space.
The man in the basement had sex almost daily.
The woman in the attic had panic attacks.
The man in the basement had only one rule:
the woman in the attic was banned from his bedroom.
But once she stole in and lay on his bed
in his absence (or perhaps he was absent because she was there).
The man in the basement moved to the West Coast;
the woman in the attic crossed the Atlantic,
whereas the house with the attic and basement saw states
of fumigation, exorcism, detoxification, and rehabitation.

Jesus with Cigarette

Michael said there was a painting of Jesus
smoking a cigarette, maybe by Giotto, in Rome.
I had never been to Rome but there I was
and it could have been Peckham, which has a garage
sometimes used for installations. Nowhere
could I find this old-master Jesus with cigarette. I rang
Michael, a smoker, to say I could not find the Jesus.
He laughed. Gabriel, a former smoker, was next to me
and also laughed. Gabriel said, *Michael was pulling
your leg!* Michael said, *We are Jesus. You are the painter.*

It was Discovered that Gut Bacteria were Responsible

It was discovered that gut bacteria were responsible
for human dreams. Each bacterium was entitled to pay
a fee in the form of mitochondrial energy to purchase
a 'dream token' to be dropped into a Potential Well. These
'tokens' were converted to synaptic prompts and transported
to the human brain in no particular order. So a 'token' for a
'baseball dream' deposited in the well when the human host
was aged 8 might only be used by the brain when the host
was 44, and this dream that might have been pleasant for an
8-year-old could instead emerge as a nightmare for a woman
on the brink of menopause who might worry about her
appearance in a baseball uniform, or who no longer recalled
how to hold a baseball glove and catch a ball in the field.

Catherine and Her Wheel (I)

Catherine, who was a saint, was inseparable from her wheel. She carried it everywhere, including on dog walks and visits to the old people's home. She slept next to it in bed.

Her boyfriend said, 'Sometimes I feel that you and your wheel are the couple whereas I am a third wheel.'

Catherine replied, 'Do you know how long this wheel has been in my family? Since we were primates – that's how long. One day it will belong to my children.'

What Women Want

After my best friend read a self-help book called *Make Your Own Fairy Tale* in which the author advises you to write your wish in a notebook and store it in the drawer of your bedside table, I did exactly that. One day my other half said, 'For fuck's sake I don't understand what you want.' When I suggested he look at the notebook in the bedside table, where my wish had been collecting dust for 3 years, he revealed he would never look at someone's private notebook, he was above that, and that was the end of the conversation.

DAWN CHORUS
in the style of the Medea, *with Haiku*

BIRD 1: Her husband is rich –

BIRD 2: She abandoned her children –

BIRD 3: Her family is Turkish, maybe they're Greek –

BIRD 4: She never fit in here –

BIRD 1: The husband is Danish, the husband left –

BIRD 2: Her husband won't leave her –

BIRD 3: Some country that practises honour killings –

BIRD 4: She was sectioned –

BIRD 1: He has a lover, the husband left –

BIRD 2: Her husband won't leave her –

BIRD 3: Her parents don't know –

BIRD 4: Sectioned for strapping a bomb on her back –

BIRD 1: The husband left –

BIRD 2: Her husband won't leave her –

BIRD 1: He has a lover –

BIRD 2: She lives with her partner –

BIRD 4: She was a threat –

BIRD 1: He has a flat – 'separate lives'

BIRD 3: Where is his flat?

BIRD 1: In Notting Hill –

BIRD 3: In Notting Hill?

BIRD 2: No Maida Vale –

BIRD 3: The family home?

BIRD 4: She's a threat to herself and the children

pause

BIRD 1:
Do not cry, woman
You're not the first or last bird
To be forsaken.

BIRD 2:
Be ashamed, woman
What foolish and selfish bird
Could leave her own young?

BIRD 3:
We, your ancestors,
Abhor your newfangled ways;
Destruction awaits.

BIRD 4:
Does anyone know
Which narrative is correct?
They are all different.

The Adulteress

was her joke name for herself though
unfashionable & (except in the literal
sense) incorrect. She had to stop
attending dinner parties as someone
would inevitably say something
like, 'I didn't know which husband to
expect tonight!' or 'Your husband' this/
'Your husband' that with her partner
sitting right there. She did not view herself
as a joke & yet this joke word 'adulteress'
was in her head so she said to her daughter
who was learning to sew, 'Can you make
a big red A & sew it on my black dress?'
Her daughter said, 'Which black dress?'
& the woman said, 'Every black dress.'

Poem in which I Reside in a Female Prison with Two Male Guards and No Allies

My sentence was to end in May, but the law changed, and although no one can satisfactorily explain how this amendment applies to me, I am admittedly deaf to cultural nuance, insisting (as though anyone cares) that I'd have been released if I were jailed in my home country where my crime is de rigueur and where, too, my guards would almost certainly not be men, one of whom fucks me which is fine because I am *that* needy, whereas the other wants no sex but gives presents I can't use like ponchos saying *Beati Possidentes*. When new prisoners join they cursorily look my way then ignore me as though my ageing reminds them of what they'll be after 10 years of dichotomous treatment. They don't ask my advice which is just as well because I know nothing and suffer from a brain fog that is either anxiety or else I am being poisoned: maybe by the gifts from the second prison guard or maybe by the semen from the first, or maybe – as is the predominant explanation – I am administering it myself.

Scarlet Letter *Couplets*

Hester Prynne passed through her ordeal,
watched with moral zeal.

What imagination is irreverent enough to surmise
the weight of a thousand unrelenting eyes?

Hester Prynne had this dreadful agony in feeling.
With a faint ruddiness upon the walls and ceiling,

she took the baby on her arm with a burning blush.
'Hush now, gossips. Hush, Hester. Hush, child – hush.'

Ghastly scenery around her, a home and comfort nowhere,
even thus early had the child saved her from Satan's snare.

He had won a distinguished name
such as must always invest the spectacle of guilt and shame:

'Thou and thine, Hester Prynne, belong to me –
live, therefore, and bear about thy doom with thee!'

'Thou wilt go!' said Hester calmly, as he met her
with only that one ornament – the scarlet letter.

Ashley Madison Couplets

Ashley Madison is the most open-minded dating community.
For women, Ashley Madison is free.

Millions of people like you are looking for a discreet connection.
Millions are drawn to the site because they want discretion.

No matter your reason, you'll find what's missing at Ashley
    Madison,
originally designed specifically for married men and women.

You control exactly what you want people to see.
We know you value your privacy.

It's Not Her Story to Tell

The famous novelist and not-so-famous poet, long time colleagues in the same English department, never had a real conversation until they both landed a residential course in Rome, during which the famous novelist, who had just finalised a bitter divorce, felt fragile enough to talk about her life, and the poet, who was feeling chatty himself, told his autobiography over grappa and ice. The next year the famous novelist published a book in which the main character was a not-so-famous poet who had the same life experiences as the not-so-famous poet in Rome. Outraged, the not-so-famous poet texted an even-less-famous poet who had never been to Rome but who had once complimented the famous novelist on her leather jacket at the departmental Christmas party. 'Can you believe she wrote *my* story?' he typed. 'It's not her story to tell.' The even-less-famous poet replied, 'Isn't that awful!'

The H Man

His superpower was being the subject of ever-taller tales
about his prowess at hurling, a sport with prehistoric Gaelic
origins where players use hurleys (sticks) on a sliotar (ball),
aiming it over the crossbar of the goalpost for 1 point,
or under the crossbar of the goalpost & into the net for 3.
Considered to be 'the fastest player ever' in a sport known
to be 'the world's fastest field sport', the H Man once broke
the nose of an opponent with his force plus his velocity
(though some say he broke his ribs or legs). He did not
'go professional' because hurling remains an amateur sport,
but he did become a poet because that profession does exist.

Catherine and Her Wheel (II)

After a few years of marriage, it became clear to her husband that Catherine was less a saint than a *victim*. As in, everyone had wronged her. Meanwhile the spikey wheel became a hazardous object of rivalry among their young children. Catherine's husband basically became Jesus in order to cope.

He joked, 'I'm changing my name to Jesus!'

The children asked, 'What's "Jesus"?'

'I'm Jesus,' he said. 'That's what Jesus is.'

Dear Fellow Parents

Whilst our sons prepare assiduously for the contest,
I thought I might send a note concerning how we,
their parents, can usefully support & aid them.
In short, expect the unexpected in terms of weather.
Nottingham is rightly notorious for howling gales
& extreme temperatures: hypothermia & sunburn
are possible, frequently in the same weekend.
Send your son with layers & more layers.
You, too, will need layers because clothes
which are wet tend to stay wet. The tent
contains tables, chairs, a barbecue, kettle,
hungry & thirsty boys, coaches, parents
& the occasional sibling or two. SPACE
IS LIMITED. If your son has a life-threatening
allergy, please flag this, though we have not had
a 'no nuts' policy hitherto. If you are not sure
what to bring, think what your son might like to eat
& multiply the quantity by, say, eight.
Could we have specific offers of the following?
Tea bags, Horlicks, hummus, two gas canisters
(Stoker family, may I prevail upon you?);
a super-sized cooler (Bernz-Joneses?);
duck wraps (please could you commit to several
dozen in recognition of the unique place
these wraps hold in our hearts); flapjacks
(popular with certain coaches); lemon drizzle cake
(popular with me!); bottled water & industrial
quantities of rubbish bags. A couple of pointers,
if I may, to families who may not have attended before:
for three hours before the event, your son
won't be able to eat protein, but must stay fuelled
with light carbs. After the competition,

the feeding frenzy commences:
parents will be pressed into grilling & serving
more food than one would consider possible.
Feeding & cleaning take place continuously.
But the rewards are peerless, a spectacle –
without fear of exaggeration, the most important
contest for us as a whole. Let's see
if we can have another memorable weekend.
I am likely to be wearing something pink.

Report Card: Classics

AUTUMN

When she is in the spotlight, she produces
the goods satisfactorily enough.
She is not a committed Hellenist
it has to be said
which is a shame but not shameful.

*

SPRING

The focus and drift of my comments have not changed
in the brief interval since they were written.
If I stand over her with a weapon
of mass destruction she does what she has to –
but I would rather not.

The House of Atreus

Electra

I am signing none of the emails with an 'x' because
whatever affection he feels for me is not being
transferred. Affection is not a currency. I can't
make him feel affection just as he is failing to make
me feel affection. I am anxious about my appointment
with the GP though I feel better than I did last year
and the year before. I arrived Saturday. The flight
was fine except for snafus at JFK: immigration queues,
misplaced bags, then Orestes didn't turn up
so I hailed a taxi. We got lost because I don't know the way
from the Northern State Parkway. Dad scolded the driver
for lacking a GPS then gave him $100, which sums up
my dad: first the meanness and then the reward.

I'M OBSESSED WITH MY HEALTH WHICH I GUESS

Clytemnestra

I'm obsessed with my health, which I guess is a capitalist
construct. I put a codicil in my will in case my son
is orphaned. I bought a bed with my husband's Am Ex after
my Visa was declined from overuse. The salesman misheard
the 'X' in my postcode as 'S,' so I said 'X like exit'
& Aegisthus shook his head because 'exit' doesn't really
begin with 'X'. I transferred money to my husband's account.

Iphigenia

I bought flowers on the Clifton Road
because I think I might be dead?
The severe light and wind are exactly
as they were when I was a little
girl and I wrote DANGER on an oak,
believing our branches to be
perilous & public. Once my
grandfather tried to explain the blood-
lines between me & Helen of Troy
but I don't speak good Greek so he may
have said something else. He was the only
man who ever loved me & offered
to be buried with me but I said no
I said I would be married with the wind.

BECAUSE I WANT TO BE AROUND NEGATIVITY

Orestes

Because I want to be
around negativity
as little as possible,
I avoid my sister,
though I wish she were more
hospitable. I've made a
scrupulous dossier of
her insanity &
I bcc my parents
on all our correspondence.
Quoting Melanie Klein,
she claims she's the family
scapegoat, when we all know she
inherited bad genes.
I'm not married to our
father, as she unattract-
ively taunts, but I do
respect his business
acumen, especially
the hotels. No one
sacrificed anyone:
my unfamilial sister
gave herself willingly to
whatever she worshipped.

Agamemnon

At family dinner we talked politics.
Electra, now 9, supports the Liberal
Democrats because her friend said they're best.
Orestes, aged 12, was visited by
constituency MPs at school and
was most impressed with the Conservatives.
When I said what I felt were the downsides
of the Conservatives, Electra cried:
she seems to have some guilt about money,
a trait she shares with my Clytemnestra.

THEN WE HAD THE BEST MEAL OF OUR STAY

Clytemnestra

Then we had the best meal of our stay,
a place you could pass without noticing,
a small establishment with a single woman
serving a whole room of diners & I wept
as we ate, *I have felt so fretful for so*
many years, not believing I'm loved.
He countered with his own frustration:
our constitutional differences.
I tried again: *I want us to be*
a family or I'll go back to my
original one. When we left, the
proprietress kissed us on both cheeks.
[I'm constricted on this Eurostar,
two bags at my feet & suffering from wine.]

SHE'S A PAIN IN THE ARSE BUT SHE'S NICE TO LOOK AT [VARIATIONS]

Aegisthus

she's a pain
in the arse
but she's nice
to look at

she's a pain
in the arse
but she's (still)
nice looking

at 40
she's a pain
but she's loyal
and nice

she gets pains
I'm patient
I'm nice
she says

I'm an arse
I want sex
with the daughter
of my ex

WE HAD A BIG ROW YESTERDAY

Iphigenia

We had a big row yesterday:
I was agitated because
he keeps mentioning the self-harm
in such a selfish way, as though
to slice up my veins was violent
to *him.* When I asked him to drop
it, he claimed I want to 'control'
him. As I left, I shouted, *Why
can't we just be together?* He
said, *So I can live in this hell
all the time?* and I said *On the
contrary* [yes I used those words]
*don't you see I'm only like this
when you leave me, which is always.*

I

The P Man

His superpower was launching the careers of mainly
female potters, first by detecting talent in pensioners
he instructed in adult education programmes; later
by inviting younger potters to classes at his home,
a known arena of drinking and swiving. Apropos
of swiving, he appreciated what he termed 'big women':
one was a recovering alcoholic palace librarian
whose youth, he said, 'flattered him'; another ran off
and married a different man only days after her last
physical encounter with the P Man, leaving the latter
to view himself, simultaneously, as exploited and alone.

Information from the Headmaster

As you know, there was an incident on the river last week.
One of our Fifth Form crews, the J14 Octuple, got caught
on some moorings below Chiswick Pier. When the boat sank,
one boy went into the water but Mr S was able to pull
him into the launch. A second boy found refuge on the cruiser.
Mr S did a headcount, then dropped the rescued boy at the pier.
Rowing on the river is of course a potentially hazardous activity.
However, Mr S and the Boat House Staff are experienced
oarsmen with deep knowledge of the Thames and its ways.

I've Had a Positional Headache for Two Months

I've had a positional headache for two months &
a brain tumour is suspected so I will have an MRI.
I feel I have been killing myself, though the truth lies
in between. As drinking is the one thing that
predictably exacerbates my headaches, I stopped.
Sometimes when I have binge-drunk, the pressure
at the top of my head is so great that I hallucinate,
like the time I thought Pascale had taken over my body.
These 'glitch' moments are worrisome, like my certainty
there was a mirror in the kitchen (there never was) and that
doors once on my right now stand, to mock me, on my left.

All the Signs were There

She asked 'Whatever'   for a sign – a pagan deity,
a Confucian ancestor,   a Talmudic advisor,
an angular Greek   Orthodox saint –
that this man   and his agrarian world
loved her.   First there was the storm
that blew down the shed   and killed the prize horse.
Then a fallen arcade   of trees made passage
to the house impossible.   Then the sheep began to bleat
'Bad!' repeatedly.   Then the sky produced
a scroll that said,   *Avaunt! and quit my sight!*
Because her vision   was less than perfect
and so was her hearing   she stayed for a very long time.

Ladies' Voices

CURTAIN RAISER

Everyone has gone
But the barbecue is here. Is someone coming back for it?
William is going back for it tomorrow
Ah that belongs to William. William is going back tomorrow
What a successful weekend overall

Did anyone see a white china salad bowl
I'm looking for a plastic container with a red strip around the edge
Weren't we fortunate with the weather
Weren't we lucky
Wow what a race
What a race indeed

ACT II

Accident on the M4 by the exit to the M25
We're stuck in it too
We are through
I'm driving Rupert, Henry & the dog
Are you there yet?
You will be fine, I was caught too
The rain is driving at an angle
Where are you all?
We're all here, where are you?

ACT III

First Brexit, now this
What a week, so sad
I feel the way I did last Friday, totally bereft
Those boys are lucky with their great British strengths
Calm under pressure, humility & humour
Nick was telling us how he read *The Odyssey*

That will stand them in good stead

ACT IV

What a shame, big loss
It's a very difficult time
Equally painful
I saw them laughing

SCENE II

His father has been given one month to live
He's not ill at all
Does anyone have Nurofen?
Oh dear, was it raining?

Gosh I will miss it, and you, very much
Congratulations and best wishes for the future
What a fabulous memory
Wasn't it just such a special and wonderful occasion
The baton is well and truly passed

Here is the Official Line on Attire

Gentlemen must wear lounge suits,
ladies must wear dresses with a
hemline below the knee, no trousers
of any description. Hats are customary
but not essential. Cash and cards
may be used for refreshments.
This extraordinary spectacle is one
of the best things Britain has given
the world: civilized conduct on land,
absolute brutality on the water.

Break-up Letter

First of all, I'm 49. I am unable to love in my life as best I can.
I loved you often one time. I was very scared: intimacy
meant forever. From May 2009 to December 2010
I was married to eggshells. (I am still working on that able love.)
But I woke up at that point, I tried to make promises I couldn't keep.
I'm not sure what you said: *Work on this while being with me* or *Go*.
You were trapped with times of great happiness, so I walked,
scared of your trust. Irrational and unreasonable, time terrified me.
I wasn't happier with the relationship than I was. If I told you
I loved you, you would think I wasn't sure I could love you.

I'm sorry I didn't communicate better while we were together
but it always felt very real to me when you were often angry.
I felt your just anger. I put it all down to your friends and the fact
that I can't change this, or anyone, forever. I always told you
I didn't want to get it. I like people together *and* one-on-one,
but I also like being distrustful and never certain of my love.
The day I broke up with you, I broke up with you because
I loved you enough. This didn't seem to make you happy.
I'm not saying my responses are correct but they are my
safe course. I'm a confused person and I hope you move on.

Singles Cruise

It was a singles cruise but it wasn't a singles cruise:
each participant simulated detachment but none
was actually single. Some, like the recently widowed,
were attached to ghosts. Others were legally attached
to a living person they once but no longer loved.
A surprising number loved their partners profoundly
while fearing said partners inhabited the category
of those who loved them no longer. These participants,
whose fears may or may not have been well founded,
attempted self-protection by labelling themselves single.
Soon a pattern emerged: those who feared abandonment
developed around them a planetary-like orbit
of potential new partners to whom they could not attach
because they were already attached. Such orbits lasted,
sometimes, for years. The orbiters went to self-help groups
and/or analysts and/or wrote letters to advice columnists.
Because they could not detach from their objects of unrequited
affection, they became the predominant clientele for future
singles cruises, unilaterally sustaining the singles cruise business.

How to be a Dream Girl not a Doormat about the 'Ex'

While the Doormat asks neurotic questions about his ex,
the Dream Girl looks at her watch if her man brings up the ex,
and if the man ever says, 'Everyone was in love with my ex'
a Dream Girl won't ask for a photo, but if a photo of the ex
is provided, the Dream Girl won't demean the appearance of the ex
because her man will likely rush to his ex's
defence. The lesson is that when a man considers his ex
a prize looks have little to do with it, for when a woman acts
like a prize a man can forget he's with a battleaxe.
What should you say when he asks questions about *your* ex?
Remember you're a prize, so you needn't report that your ex
stole appliances or defaulted on child support or that your ex
has a Mafioso brother doing time for racketeering or that your ex
is 'still stalking you' – because your man will not find these ex
stories charming, if he's classy, so what you say about your ex
is simply, 'We wanted different things' or, alternatively, 'My ex
and I went separate ways.' It's none of his business: your ex
and all the vicissitudes of your past, like the jewellery your ex
gave you which you pawned, or your violent fantasies about your ex
because inquiring minds *don't* need to know. Did you know that exes
are a common conversation topic among men: 'You remember my ex,
the one who snapped . . . ?' they might say, referring to the 'terrible' ex
who was 'possessed by demons' thus causing the inevitable ex-
tramarital affair? Of course he *never* had anything to do with his ex's
transformation, he was a perfect angel, but lo and behold, the ex-
orcist was suddenly required! Women believe these narratives and ex-
coriate themselves if they're Doormats, but love is beset by variables,
and Dream Girls must take control in this world of unknowns.

The A Man

His superpower was achieving the world's first happy marriage
by wedding his daughter, whom he loved at first sight
i.e. when she was adopted at the age of 6 by the woman
he was wooing & whose inevitability in the girl's life
led him to stick around until the girl was a preteen, a reedy
netball star in the making whose long legs under her
polyester shorts gave him a semi-permanent hard-on
that he translated into practised looks of empathy & affection
which all girls need to properly grow & so she grew
to adore this man like the New Testament God & it came to pass
that, once of legal age, she entered his sagging bed & stayed there.

Ooga-Booga *Cento*

after Frederick Seidel

A naked woman my age is a total nightmare.
When the doctor told me that I could have died
(what could be more pleasant than talking about people dying?)
which is dangerous, which I do not like.
I go to Carnegie Hall.
The joy is actually terrible.

Under an exophthalmic sky of stars
and a flock of Japanese schoolgirls waiting to be fucked,
I sense your disdain, darling.
Civilized life is actually about too much.
I am no longer human.
The crocodile king is dead.

There was a Will but There was No Way

It was a legal will but there was no way: the executor loathed the wife, for the executor was an ex of the deceased, and exes don't like being replaced.

The wife said hello. The executor said hello also, but in a way that wasn't very nice to the wife. 'How's the career?' she added.

The wife admitted there was no career: she had never gotten the prize.

The ex already knew the wife had not gotten the prize, and had no career, because the ex was both a winner and a judge of the prize.

The wife got the man but didn't get the prize. The ex got the prize but didn't get the man. Together they could have had everything.

The executor and the wife sifted through the dead man's papers, which included the prize.

The papers went to the Archive. The Archive sealed the papers for many years as per the conditions of the will.

When the papers emerged, so did the squabbles, for the papers revealed discord.

The biographers and the readers aligned themselves with one side or the other. A libretto was written, and the opera was entered for the prize.

Anyway Something Happened

Anyway something happened
& even the colour of the bedroom
changed from red & blue to hunter
green or something *warlike*
& I hardly recognized the room
for a split second & felt like a moth
on a wooden ledge (with my wings).

Never on a Sunday

The hummingbird takeover had its turning
point in Athens, when four hummingbird
businessmen demanded to meet with the CEO
of AΔMI, an ancient power company, on a Sunday,
an action forbidden by the Byzantine church which,
though no longer dominant by the secular 21st c.,
remained 'in the DNA' of the Greek people. It is unclear
if the hummingbirds purchased AΔMI, but the breach
of the 'Never On a Sunday Law' was the beginning
of the end: the hummingbirds infiltrated high-tax
residential areas of greater New York, obtained cases
of Château Lafite at auction, and secured an alternative
to the Panama Canal. Films from the 20th c. that had
extrapolated world rule by Russians dressed as Martians
were rendered 'dated'; and those unpopular citizens
who had predicted the rise of the hummingbirds
were retroactively named prophets and saints.

The Death of Empiricism

When you think someone is a sadist, it may mean that you are a masochist.

You can never know if a photo of the president with a dog has been faked, whether in the 'Photoshop' sense or the psychological sense.

If a spring flower blooms in December it may mean we are fucked but, equally, if a flower blooms in April we may be fucked in that instance too.

If Shakespeare wrote about a woman dressed as a man dressed as a woman dressed as a man, perhaps he wasn't considering gender at all.

Your fear of abandonment above every other condition may have emerged because you are a deserter.

Someone who makes the gestures of love may not love you, and someone who makes none of the gestures but behaves in a loving way also may not love you.

Difference is initially exciting, but ultimately more exciting is finding any thing in which you can see your self.

What looks like the flag of Japan may be a bloodied bed sheet; and an attempted mating call may rouse only those of the wrong sex.

Power is a superficial state, but a superficial state (e.g. one that erects empty villages) is not likely to be powerful, except when it possesses a hydrogen bomb.

Humility may seem like good medicine, but it makes the organism – and those organisms attached to it – weak.

The flipside of a close-knit family is an honour killing.

Someone who hisses when you offer her food is not the snake you want in your house when the apocalypse comes.

That your daughter asks for a glass of milk while you are reading her this poem does not mean it is without sustenance.

Demon

'Good news,' said the doctor, 'it's a demon.'
I asked for its name: was it No One?
Was it Superego? He said it wasn't those
but he couldn't guess the name. 'Who knows,'
he said, 'It mightn't even be a demon.
It's what we call a "diagnosis by elimination".'
Explaining he couldn't operate,
the doctor said let's go ahead and medicate
the hell out of it, make it sleepy.
I named him 'Demon' after his identity.
I put him to sleep twice a day, one short,
one long; three times a week he did sport;
he grew to six foot two; I said he was good;
I went to the door of his room and left food.

Object

for Suki's dress

Your name shall be governed by your owner not your
provenance. You shall be pregnant or empty of flesh.
People may rise for you in public transport, or watch
you hang in the Calle Giazzo. Of you someone will say
This delicate zephyr of a thing stirs us to the soul! while
another decrees *Let your adorning be the hidden person
of the heart.* You will walk with an elastic step; you will
be marred by no shadow of a spot. Under you will occur
12 optional sex acts and the first spasms of an exiting
new-born girl who at age 20 will resemble Africa but at 60
will be likened to Siberia – and loved and abhorred accordingly.
Though you shall have one maker, you will have at least two
possessors. While one travels to a communist state with a
serenaded leader, the other will have interludes of
agoraphobia. Through them you will see bodegas and hedges
and sheds; hares and wrens; basilicas and synagogues.
You will know frost, rain, and hurricanes, along with corporate
mammals who fake empathy. You will take the shape of
your owners, as they of you – as they once took the shape of
difficult fathers, and then took lovers who were happier 'free'.
O worthless object, love them as they have loved you, the common
skin of a female friendship. Love them even as they love or slay
or are slain; love them even as Rome burns and the
emperor does nothing but play his imperious instrument.

L'Enfer

As in life, she was a pain in the arse
in death. He could hear her roaring
all the way from the fifth circle,
'Why the hell do you get to be in a
better circle than me, I'm wrathful
because of your lust –' A gust of wind
blew him to a different part of the
second circle where communication
with the fifth was impossible. A man
spoke to him commiseratively:
'We have to listen to those cows
for eternity. It's their moaning keeps
the furnaces lit.' He blew away again,
revelling in each brief moment of
freedom when the wind changed.
When there was time he wrote poems;
when he didn't have ideas he practised
writing in dialects he had little
familiarity with. Soon hell was filled
with his scribblings wafting from circle
to circle in ascending order, then
burning in the furnace (which indeed
was fuelled by his wife) and wafting
away again in their final form, as ash.

Catherine and Her Wheel (III)

When my teachers grew old and died, when my friends
went sparer and sparer, when small islands suffered
from the New Weather, when my children found me
offensively morbid, when my looks officially went,
when my enemies became friends became rivals became
allies became masters became servants until we lacked
energy for anything even escape from our celebrated
cities whose skylines transitioned from greatness to perfect
meaninglessness as when a person loses her mind
like my cohorts who were going crazier and crazier until
I wondered *Is this sensitive ageing? What the fuck
is going on here?* . . . I knew nothing, and the nothing I knew
was more profoundly nothing even than the nothing
we know at our rarest bottommost humblest moments
because usually we know *one* thing – we know
we're not dead or that 'apple' has a feminine article in French,
but this was *absolute zero* like when the saint fell off a horse
then into a coma then woke up and said to another saint
that there was *nothing*, that there was *'nada de nada'*,
the most perfect Spanish expression, the most beautiful
and poetic circle, the nothing wheel,
the wheel I have carried through all routes of my life, the wheel
I was fundamentally wedded to, my true beloved,
watch me touch it now look at it look at it: nothing.

ACKNOWLEDGEMENTS

Thank you to the editors of these journals, anthologies, etc. for publishing poems in this collection: *3am magazine*, *Agenda*, *Bristow* (artist catalogue for Adel Abdessemed), *Fence*, *Granta*, *Magma*, *The Nation*, *The New Statesman*, *Penguin Modern Poets 5*, *Ploughshares*, *Poems in Which*, *Poetry*, *Poetry London*, *Poetry Wales*, *Swimmers*, *tender*, *Test Centre 8*, *The Best British Poetry 2015*, *The Forward Book of Poetry 2017*, *The Poetry Review*, *Traverse Poetry Trading Cards* (Stonewood Press), BBC Radio 3's *The Verb*, and *Writing Motherhood* (Seren). Other poems appeared in a pamphlet, *2008*, edited by Sam Riviere of If a Leaf Falls Press.

Thank you to my editor Donald Futers of Penguin UK; and to Harriet Moore of David Higham Associates.

Thank you to editors, friends and curators for commissions: Rachael Allen, Hannah Barry, Sophie Collins, Juliette Desorgues (the ICA), S. J. Fowler, Jacqueline Gabbitas, Carolyn Jess-Cooke, Martin Parker, and especially Edward Doegar, whose assignment on behalf of The Poetry Society and The British Museum resulted in 'The House with Only an Attic and a Basement' and, ultimately, this book.

Thank you to friends, colleagues, students, supervisors and others who offered editorial help, inspiration, friendship or support, especially Nuar Alsadir, Katherine Angel, Louise Bangay, Simon Barraclough, Emily Berry, Kate Bingham, Frederic N. Busch, John Canfield, Gerry Cambridge, Jessica Clark, Geraldine Clarkson, Josh Cohen, Cathleen Allyn Conway, Sasha Dugdale, Linda Gregerson, Catherine Hamilton, Vera Iliatova, Phil Hancock, Emily Hasler, Martha Kapos, Amy Key, Suki Kim, Sunny Kim, Phillis Levin, Patrick Mackie, Jamie McKendrick, Melissa Ozawa, Rebecca Perry, Rachel Piercey, Mischa Foster Poole,

Neville Purssell, Declan Ryan, Don Share, Kathryn Simmonds, Tom Sleigh, Dorota Sowala-Roshdy, Martha Sprackland, George Szirtes, The Poetry School, Jack Underwood, Megan Virtue, Estela V. Welldon, Matthew Welton, Aime Williams, Chrissy Williams and Hugo Williams.

Love and particular thanks to my family for tolerating apparent likenesses between themselves and certain characters in these fictions; and also to Maurice Riordan, who helped with every aspect of this book.

NOTES AND ATTRIBUTIONS

'ABC' borrows phrases from Sigmund Freud.

'DAWN CHORUS in the style of the *Medea*, with Haiku' is particularly indebted to Rachel Cusk's version of *Medea*.

The rhyming text in '*Scarlet Letter* Couplets' is derived from rearranged passages in Nathanial Hawthorne's *The Scarlet Letter*; the text from the Ashley Madison couplets was found on the Ashley Madison website in 2016.

'Dear Fellow Parents' and 'Here Is the Official Line on Attire' are edited versions of emails by Madeleine Plaut.

'Ladies' Voices' is modelled after a Gertrude Stein playlet by the same name; the overheard voices are from a WhatsApp group.

'How to be a Dream Girl not a Doormat about the "Ex"' borrows the 'Dream Girl' versus 'Doormat' concept from Sherry Argov's *Why Men Love Bitches*, and repurposes some of Argov's phrases.

'*Ooga-Booga* Cento' is made from lines from Frederick Seidel's *Ooga-Booga*.

'Object' contains a short phrase by Sigmund Freud, another by Marianne Moore, and another from the First Epistle of Peter.